Twenty Ways To Pop The Question

Present Jewelry For All Occasions With Romantic Imagination

By David W. Richardson, CSP
and Jean M. Means

Twenty Ways to Pop the Question
Present Jewelry For All Occasions With Romantic Imagination

By David W. Richardson, CSP and Jean M. Means

Published by:
Janisue Publishing
10410 E. Cholla
Scottsdale, AZ 85259

Printing 2001, 2002, 2003, 2004, 2005, 2006, 2007

ISBN: 0-9708281-0-1
Printed in the United States of America

Foreword

When it comes to romance, guys, quite often we just don't get it. Dates like Valentine's Day, birthdays, and even anniversaries sometimes don't seem that important to us . . . much to our regret, we simply fail to remember them.

Women start planning for their wedding when they are still little girls and one of the single most important moments in a woman's life is when you get down on your knee and ask her to marry you. She will never, ever forget that day . . . nor will she ever forget how you carefully created a very special moment in her life.

This book is written to help you create a beautiful proposal of marriage or a romantic Valentine's Day, birthday, anniversary, or Christmas that she will treasure for a lifetime. It doesn't have to be really fancy, nor does it have to be expensive. Women don't really care how much you spend; they care about how much you care.

So, as you read through these heartwarming stories, give some serious thought to how you can create a romantic event with the greatest of love, care, and deep sincerity.

We may not be born romantic, but we can learn.

Make it happen.
Dave

Now for the Woman's Point of View . . .

Ahhhhhh, romance. We thrive on it. If you only knew the dried roses we've bundled lovingly with ribbon to remind us of those times you made us feel so special. And don't even ask about the saved cards, love notes, play programs . . . I could go on, but I'm sure you get the picture.

Women love to feel special. And, face it, guys! If the woman you love feels special, she makes you feel special too. So, surprise her! Do something fun and exciting that makes both of you feel good.

And I have to echo what Dave said: "Women don't really care about how much you spend; they care about how much you care." It's your caring that makes her feel loved and special.

These stories are basic stepping stones to help you to become creative about giving gifts. You'll have fun, she'll have fun, and the whole world will see you together and know how happy you make each other.

Best of romance to you!
Jean

Contents

An Airplane Full of Roses

A young man boarded a plane for Dallas with a huge armful of beautiful red roses. He was on his way to ask the love of his life to marry him.

As he walked down the airplane aisle, he handed each passenger a rose and showed them a picture of his fiancé-to-be who would be meeting him at the gate.

At his request, as each passenger left the plane upon landing they walked up to the surprised and curious young woman and handed her a rose with a word or two of good wishes. When her arms were full of roses the passengers began laying the rest of them around her feet.

With his fellow passengers gathered in a semi-circle around her, all beaming with pleasure, the young man walked up to his love, knelt on one knee, presented her with a beautiful diamond ring, and asked her to be his wife.

Angel in the Choir

Singing in the choir at my church is a passion of mine made even more wonderful by the fact that my future husband is the choir director. We met the first night I attended choir practice and had an enthusiastic discussion about music choices appropriate for our church and our large choir's capabilities.

Every week we meet to practice for the upcoming Sunday services. We sing at three services on Sunday and are all very dedicated to the successful creation of a service filled with uplifting, well-executed music. Peter and I had hit it off that very first night and not only enjoyed seeing each other at practice and church, but spent a lot of our spare time together as well. Before we knew it we were considered "a couple".

Christmas at the church is especially exciting, but the behind-the-scenes work it takes to create a wonderful holiday celebration filled with joyous voices usually leaves us time for little else. My second year in the choir found me running around like a maniac trying to squeeze in shopping, baking, and gift wrapping between all of the extra practices we were having. I knew, of course, that all of the practicing would be worth it in the end, but little did I know just how special it would turn out.

Christmas morning came and the choir was bustling around the dressing room decked out in crisp red and white robes. Peter was rushing around like a red blur as he gave last minute instructions and reminded everyone of their cues for solos and Bible readings. I smiled as I watched him and wondered when we'd have enough time to celebrate Christmas ourselves, just he and I.

We filed solemnly into the church before many parishioners had arrived and began a beautiful rendition of "Silent Night". I lost myself in the wonderful Christmas music as we moved from one song to the next. Peter stood at the front gently guiding us, a satisfied smile on his face.

The church was nearly full, Father had come to the side of the choir, and we all began to sing very softly. Father nodded at Peter, but what happened next was not what anyone in that church was expecting.

Peter leaned toward the microphone at his left and said, "Before we begin this celebration today, I ask that you all join me in a celebration of my own." As he said this, he was looking right up at me. I felt butterflies in my stomach as he continued.

"On this special day, I want to share my joy in finding the woman I want to share my life with. So, if Jean would come down here for a moment, I'd like to ask her to be my wife." My knees were shaking as I walked down through the choir to join Peter at the front of the congregation. He knelt before me and took my hand.

"Jean, in front of the people who care about us most, I ask you to be my wife," he said as he slid a fabulous diamond ring on my finger. The whole congregation seemed to be leaning forward to hear my whispered "Yes" as Peter rose to give me a hug.

I could barely walk back to my place in the choir, and my voice was shaking so much I could only mouth the words for the rest of the service. What an incredible Christmas gift!

Baseball Fan

George had been a major league baseball fan all of his life. Every opportunity to latch onto a few tickets found George in his favorite seat — first seat, second row, right behind first base.

In the three years he had been seeing Mary he had never been able to interest her in going to one of the games. She didn't like the traffic, she didn't like the crowds, and she was content with hearing about the excitement of the game from George when he got home.

Determined to share a game with Mary, George secured a pair of tickets, handed them to her with a bow, and said, "Tomorrow afternoon, please be my guest at the game." With a cute little "you won this time, buster" smile, she finally gave in.

Mary was very taken by all the activity . . . the vendors, crowd reaction, airplanes flying overhead trailing colorful banners, and, of course, the athletes on the field.

As the seventh inning was drawing to a close, Mary glanced up to see what bright banner was flying overhead and was amazed to see "Mary, will you marry me? I love you. George" flying through the sky.

Mary did a double take, turned to George with wide eyes, and saw him beside her on his knee, left hand extended and right hand poised to put a beautiful diamond engagement ring on her finger.

The inning had come to an end, and behind George, Mary was amazed to see the players on the field lined up on the first base line waving their hats as she told him, "Yes, I'd love to be your wife." The organist burst into "Here Comes the Bride" and George's baseball buddies who had all been seated nearby rushed up to congratulate both of them with beer and hot dog toasts!

A new baseball fan had just been born!

Coffee Shop Chaos

*E*very Saturday morning, without fail, my sister Joanne and I meet for coffee at our favorite café. When the weather is nice we sit outside, and the waitress who has been serving us for years brings us our order without even having to ask us what we want. We have comfort food and girl talk, and it's the highlight of my week.

So, it was Saturday morning, we were re-hashing the week's events, and I found myself voicing the same old lament . . . that my boyfriend of three years was never going to make a serious commitment to our relationship. At 45, I was ready to settle into something more than just a steady weekend date.

Even though Joanne listened patiently, I sensed that she was distracted, and I finally asked her what was so interesting behind me? She leaned toward me and whispered, "Don't turn around, but there's a guy behind you with a hat and sunglasses that looks like he's trying to eavesdrop. I wonder if he's delusional and thinks he's a spy!" At that we giggled and continued our conversation in quieter tones.

A few seconds later I heard the chair behind me scrape the cement as our "spy" moved closer. This guy was definitely a kook who was much too interested in what we were saying. So I proceeded to launch into a tale of how I had met a fabulous bodybuilder earlier in the week and we were having a passionate affair. I added that I was thinking about breaking up with Thomas to run off with this new guy.

CRASH! In trying to strain to listen to what I was saying, the guy behind us actually fell over backwards, and I was so startled that I jumped up and managed to tip our whole table over — coffee, toast and all. What a mess and what a noise! Everyone on the patio was looking at us!

I turned to give this guy a piece of my mind and absolutely could not believe the sight of my Thomas righting himself and his chair and trying to maintain some small semblance of dignity. "What on earth do you think you're doing?" I yelled.

"Well, believe it or not, honey, this was a well-planned attempt to propose in a very unique and romantic way. It just didn't turn out exactly as I had planned!" With that, he pulled a diamond ring out of his pocket and took my hand.

"Janet, don't you even think about running off with some other guy! You're my girl, and I want you to be my wife! Will you marry me?"

Trying to hold back a combination of laughter and tears, I held out my hand for Thomas to slip the diamond on my finger. "Thomas, I'll call Fabio the minute I leave here and tell him the deal's off. I would love to be your wife."

Cooling Her Heels

*I*t was a beautiful day for a hike, the weather was perfect, but Peter seemed a little "out of it" today, a little aloof. Wendy figured it was because the end of the quarter was near and Peter was still short of his sales quota.

As they walked, she and Peter engaged in idle chit chat. If she mentioned anything about work, he quickly moved along to another subject.

The sound of the waterfall in the distance meant that lunch break was just around the corner. Her feet were tired and she was ready for a rest. The waterfall was Wendy's favorite place in the whole world, and she looked forward to a peaceful half an hour enjoying its beauty.

Running to the edge of the pool, she pulled off her hiking boots and let her feet slowly sink into the cool blue water. Peter joined her as they sat and shared a delicious lunch of peanut butter and jelly sandwiches. Afterwards, dozing in the sun, Wendy tried to think of a way to cheer Peter up a bit.

As they prepared to leave, Wendy slid on her socks and grabbed her boots. After cooling her heels in the stream, her boots always felt so much better on her feet. Lacing up her second boot, she noticed something strange about the shoelace. There was something hanging from it . . . a diamond ring! It was a diamond engagement ring!!

She turned to face Peter who had dropped to his knee beside her. Taking the boot from her, he removed the ring, looked lovingly into her eyes, and said, "Wendy, I love you more than anything in this world. I want to spend the rest of my life with you. Will you marry me?"

Wendy's response was a great big "Yes!" as she toppled Peter over into the grass to give him a kiss.

Falling for Him

Michael and I met in a composition class in our sophomore year of college. We struck up a conversation one afternoon as we were walking out of the classroom and continued talking until we reached my dorm. He asked if he could take me out for coffee later, and I told him I'd like that.

Our relationship just "felt right" from the very beginning, and we knew that we were meant to be together.

Michael and I had been dating for a little over a year when we began talking about moving in together. I had discussed the idea with my parents, and they weren't too crazy about it. They hadn't said "Absolutely not, young lady!" as I had expected, though, so I moved forward with my plan to move in.

The Saturday we had chosen to move was a chilly fall day with multi-colored leaves blowing everywhere. Fall is my favorite time of year, and I couldn't wait to get moved into our little apartment so we could decorate with all the seasonal colors.

As I trudged up the steps with a full armload of clothes, I looked up to see that

Michael had already hung a beautiful wreath made of red and gold leaves on our door. It was big and thick and had pine cones scattered around it. I wondered who had made it.

Pushing open the door with my foot, I walked in and complimented Michael on the wreath as I dropped my pile of clothes on the couch. "Who made that, Michael? It's beautiful."

"Believe it or not, I did . . .with a little help from your mom," was his reply.

"My mom?" I walked back out to take a closer look with Michael on my heels. The significance of the wreath on our door was much more apparent when I had a chance to look more closely. Hanging from a red ribbon in the center was a diamond engagement ring with a note attached to it.

In my mom's writing, the note read: "Honey, do you think we would've let you move in there if we hadn't known Michael was going to propose? Now, give the poor boy his answer! Love, Mom."

Michael had a huge smile on his face as if he knew exactly what my answer would be, and he was right. I gave him a great big "yes!"

Horse Sense

My boyfriend Carl and I had been dating for several years when we decided it was time for us to get married. It was pretty cut and dried, not a lot of romance or discussion. We didn't want to spend a lot of money on a ring because we were saving to buy some property where we could have a couple of horses, a dream both of us had had since childhood.

We always reserved our Saturday mornings for horseback riding at a friend's ranch, and one Saturday Carl told me to meet him extra early so we could watch the sun come up from our favorite spot.

We started our ride when it was still dark, but both of us were wide awake and looking forward to the ride. I had baked fresh cinnamon rolls the night before and brought them along with a thermos of hot coffee. The plan was to ride up into the mountains as it got light and stop in time to watch the glorious sunrise over the pasture down below.

As we rode up the trail, Carl reached over and touched my arm so tenderly it made me want to cry. I just love that man so much it hurts! I turned to smile at him and saw that he was holding a little box out toward me. We walked our horses off to the side of the trail, and I opened the box to find a precious gold ring with little diamonds all across the top. It was the most beautiful ring I had ever seen.

"Carl," I whispered, "I thought we weren't going to do this."

Carl reached over and slipped the ring on my finger as my eyes filled with tears.

"Joanne, I love you so much that I want every single person who sees you to notice that you have a ring on your finger and know that our love for each other is a special thing for us. That ring is nothing fancy, but the depth of love it carries is beyond measure. Will you be my wife?"

What a special moment in my life. That was fifteen years ago, and I'm reminded of it every time we ride our horses up that trail to watch the sunrise together.

Name That Tune

Le Francais is one of the finest restaurants in the city, very elegant, very posh, the perfect place for Michael to ask Melinda to spend the rest of her life with him.

Two weeks before popping the "big question" he met with the maitre d' of Le Francais and planned out every detail of the special evening.

The night finally arrived, and as Michael and Melinda walked into the restaurant, the maitre d' extended his hand, greeted them warmly, and immediately showed them to their special table which was adorned with beautiful flowers and exquisite tableware.

First they were served a glass of Melinda's favorite Chardonnay, then came escargot, then the soup, salad, entrée, dinner wine, dessert, and after-dinner cordial . . . all pre-ordered by Michael, all Melinda's favorites.

As they sipped their cordials, the waitstaff gathered to form a semi-circle around the table, and the strolling violinist came over and played "Isn't It

Romantic." Michael rose from the table, knelt before Melinda, and slid a dazzling diamond ring onto her finger as he said, "Will you marry me Melinda?"

The moment she said "Yes," the champagne corks popped all over the restaurant, and everyone held up their glasses in a toast to the happy couple.

Now That's a Prize!

Having dated for five years, Sue knew that it was only a matter of time before Larry popped the question. This particular Saturday afternoon found them enjoying a beautiful fall afternoon at the city zoo. Excusing himself, Larry went over and bought a couple of sodas, a bag of popcorn for himself, and for Sue, her favorite, Cracker Jacks.

Just like a little kid, she couldn't wait to find the prize hidden in the box. After every handful, she would reach deeper into the box, feeling around for that ever-famous little plastic toy. All of a sudden, a smile lit up her face . . . she'd found it. Shaking the box back and forth while wiggling her fingers inside she pulled the prize from the box, anxious to see what it was.

A look of astonishment came over her face. This wasn't a toy . . . no, this was a beautiful diamond ring. Larry pulled her to him, and as he asked her to be his bride, he carefully slid that diamond ring onto her finger.

Office Romance

My new job as assistant to the president of a large manufacturing firm proved to be challenging in a variety of ways, not the least of them my huge attraction to my boss. He was a dynamic, handsome man with so much energy and enthusiasm it was contagious for everyone in the office.

I had only been working for Ron for a couple of weeks when he suddenly seemed to slow down and take notice that I was an attractive woman. I could just tell by the way he stopped what he was doing and got all flustered when I walked into his office one afternoon that something had just "clicked". Of course, I didn't pursue it because it's common knowledge that office romances are an invitation to disaster.

Ron, however, being accustomed to great success in the business world, set his sights on me and didn't let up until I agreed to go out to dinner with him. He was subtle about it and made it a point to ask me when no one else was around, and he was just so darn cute I couldn't say no.

Our first dinner together was perfect. He took me to a beautiful restaurant with a view of the city that took my breath away. And I found Ron's company absolutely wonderful. We talked and laughed for hours without feeling the least bit self conscious. And so it began . . .

Ron and I dated each other for almost a year without anyone in the company knowing of our relationship. I truly believe that work and pleasure should be kept separate, so it wasn't all that hard to switch from one relationship during the day to the other in the evening. Both of us were quite content with the situation, or so I thought.

It was the Tuesday morning before Christmas, and I was rushing to complete a couple of deadlines before I took a few days off for the holidays. I was in deep concentration when I realized that I could hear music other than the piped-in background noise that was always playing. I strained to figure out what it was and where it was coming from. It sounded almost like bagpipes, but why would anyone be playing the bagpipes in our office building?

I went back to work but could hear the music getting nearer and nearer and, yes, I was certain it was bagpipes. I was determined not to interrupt my work but was forced to when the whole office reacted to the bagpipe player that had just walked off the elevator . . . Ron right behind him in full Scottish regalia. I couldn't believe my eyes!

The bagpipe player and Ron proceeded boldly to my desk and stopped right in front of me. I was so surprised, I didn't know how to react. And then, Ron took my hand and pulled me out from behind my desk, knelt down before me, and held out a diamond ring that made everyone gasp. Or, maybe it was the fact that the boss was proposing to his assistant that no one knew he was even dating! Either way, when Ron took my hand and slipped the ring on my finger, asking me to be his wife, I responded with a thrilled "Yes!"

On-line Romance

*F*rustrated with the inability to meet men in my world, I took a giant leap of faith and started contacting people through the singles sites I found on the Internet. I found that I could actually specify age and the city where they lived as well as view pictures of the people I found during my search. From there I could see their likes and dislikes, their philosophies on life and relationships, and a whole array of information. What could be better?

Not everyone I "met" was someone I was compatible with, but I did find one person that I particularly enjoyed corresponding with via e-mail, so much so that Tom and I decided to speak to each other on the telephone. He was a big hit with me! He was humorous, intelligent, and thoughtful, and I found myself looking forward to meeting him in person. So Tom and I met for coffee one Sunday morning and, even though this sounds like a cliché, it was love at first sight.

We both found what we had been looking for in a relationship — warmth, understanding, respect, and love. We were perfect for each other and throughout the next year developed a very strong relationship. During that time, we spent quite a bit of time at the computer, which seems rather fitting considering the way we met. Tom and his best friend, Mike, own a web site design company, and we often looked at sites in progress so I could give Tom my opinion. He's very proud of his work and so am I.

One Saturday evening Tom asked me to look at his latest site design, so we went over to his place to check it out. He had mentioned the site several times during the week, saying it was giving him some difficulty; he couldn't come up with just the right graphics to make his point the way he wanted to.

As soon as we got to his place Tom started up his computer and typed in www.Janet.com —"hmmm, strange name for a web site," I thought. Then the site came up in a burst of fireworks — it was like the most glorious Fourth of July fireworks display I had ever seen! The lights in the room dimmed above us, and I heard a champagne cork pop. "Just keep watching that screen, Janet," Tom said, so I kept my eyes glued there waiting to see what would happen next.

I watched one last burst of fireworks of every color imaginable, and then, from the screen, a hand came toward me holding a ring . . . a very spectacular diamond ring with rainbow colors glinting off of it. It was all just incredible! I laughed with delight and turned to tell Tom he is an absolute genius, and there was that very same hand holding a diamond ring toward me, only this time the hand was attached to Tom as he knelt down beside me to ask me to be his wife.

My ecstatic "Yes" was followed by a champagne toast to our future together and to the wonderful concept of computer dating . . . and engagement!

Only in the Movies

Bob and Karen spent most Saturday evenings watching old movies together at her apartment, but tonight Bob made sure things would be a bit different. With the help of a friend, Bob copied Karen's favorite classic love story, filmed himself proposing to her, and then inserted it into the video at the appropriate spot.

As they sat curled up on the couch with popcorn and tissues, the classic tale of love and romance had Karen in tears by mid-story. Love found, then love lost, and then finally the wonderful moment when the woman's true love gets down on one knee to swear his everlasting love and ask her to marry him . . . and suddenly there on the screen was Bob on bended knee, holding out a beautiful diamond ring, and asking Karen to be his wife.

Karen turned to Bob as if wondering how he could be in two places at one time, and there he was beside her on bended knee, beautiful diamond ring in hand, poised to put it on her finger as he asked her to be his wife. With tears streaming down her face, she replied with an emphatic "Yes!"

Overboard in Love

$\mathcal{M}$ark's beautiful sailboat was his pride and joy, and more often than not his sailing mate was the love of his life, Ellen. Sunshine, fluffy white clouds, and a light breeze made today a perfect day to go for a sail in the bay.

Mark's plan was to sail into a private little cove that he had discovered a few weeks earlier. It was here that he planned to take out the diamond engagement ring and ask Ellen to marry him. The champagne was on ice . . . he wanted to make this a very special day for Ellen.

Anchoring the boat, he put his plan in motion. Taking the ring out of his pocket, he called her name and began walking toward her. She saw the ring in his hand and beamed with pleasure about what was going to happen next.

As he prepared to kneel down in front of her, he slipped. He reached for the railing, the ring fell from his hand, over the side of the boat, and into the water. Both Mark and Ellen stood in stunned silence and watched as the ring quickly disappeared from view. Ellen turned to Mark with a gasp, but then said, "Well, honey, I can only hope that ring was insured!" He explained to her how much he had wanted to make this such a special day, then picked up the champagne and two glasses, saying, "It's the thought that counts, and, yes, the ring was insured."

He brought the bottle over to her but she had absolutely no interest in champagne. He said, "C'mon honey, let's celebrate our love anyway. I want you to marry me; the ring will just have to come a little later."

At the moment he was about to pour, Ellen glanced down at the glass and was startled to see a diamond ring . . . wait a minute, another diamond ring? What about the one that went overboard? She looked at Mark quizzically . . . "What are you up to buster?"

Mark smiled as he said, "The ring I dropped was straight from the dime store honey. I wanted to make a point that objects are just things. It's not a ring that makes my love for you so real and so deep, but this diamond ring I put on your finger now is an important symbol of my love for you. Will you be my wife?"

Ellen held out her hand for him to slip the ring on her finger and tearfully responded, "Mark, I would be honored to be your wife."

Pickup Proposal

*B*elieve it or not, I met my husband while driving to work one morning. He was in a big white pickup truck in the lane beside me, and we both happened to look over at each other at the same moment. Wow! He was the most handsome man I'd seen in a long time, and apparently he thought I looked pretty good too because after a few miles of flirting he gestured for me to follow him into the parking lot of my favorite local bagel shop — and I did.

Dan and I started dating that very night and were "a couple" from that point on.

When Dan and I had been seeing each other for a little over a year, I was beginning to feel like we needed to start considering making our arrangement permanent, but I didn't want to be the one to bring it up. It's a lot more fun to be proposed to than to suggest to the man in your life that you want to get married . . . so I bit my tongue and waited.

On my way to work one morning I glanced up to see what looked like Dan's pickup truck behind me, and that brought back such a pleasant rush of memories that I almost cried. Dan had sold the truck to his brother a few months earlier.

The truck started passing on my right, and I glanced over to take a closer look. Wow! What a handsome man — there was Dan behind the wheel, flirting just like he had on that first day. We smiled, we waved, and finally, instead of gesturing for me to pull over this time, Dan held up a glittering diamond ring and mouthed, "Will you marry me?"

This time I gestured for him to pull over so I could feel his arms around me when I told him, "Yes, I will marry you!"

Strike Up the Band

My fiancé James is the director of our local high school band, and he used that position to his advantage the day he proposed to me.

I work in a small office in which I'm by myself most of the time. The office is located in the center of a large parking lot that usually has very few cars in it, and I overlook that parking lot.

It was a Friday morning during football season, and as is usually the case, I could hear the marching band practicing in the distance. That was a familiar sound every day as James led his young band members in their maneuvers to be displayed at the Friday night football games.

This morning I noticed that the sound of the band was getting closer and closer. "Terrific," I thought, "sounds like I'll get to see them march by this morning." Five minutes later, sure enough, I saw the whole band rounding the corner, James in the lead.

I watched in surprise as the band turned into my parking lot and began marching into one of their formations. Only the snare drums sounded as they moved precisely into place — a giant heart formed before my eyes. They began playing "My Heart Belongs to You", and James marched smartly to the center of the heart.

James knelt down and looked up at my window where he could see me watching in amazement. First he put his hands over his heart and mouthed, "I love you Karen," and then he held a box up toward me. He opened it, and I could see that a ring glinted in the sun. At that moment, the entire band, in perfect synchronicity, shouted, "Karen, will you marry James?"

My answer was much quieter, but the beaming smile on James's face told me that he had heard my "Yes" quite clearly.

Sweet Surprise

*B*uying an engagement ring for my girlfriend Jenna was a bit overwhelming for me since I had never bought jewelry of any type for anyone. Once accomplished, I was feeling quite proud of myself until the jeweler said to me, "How do you plan to give it to her?"

"Yikes!" I thought. "Don't you just drop on one knee and say 'will you marry me?' or something like that? Well, gosh, I don't know. Any good suggestions?"

What my terrific jeweler suggested to me was so much fun and surprised Jenna so well that I wish I could do it all over again! Here's what I did:

Just down the street from the jewelry store is a café that I knew Jenna would love. With outdoor seating surrounded by blooming flowers and a canopy of trees, it had just the cozy atmosphere that she goes crazy over.

When we arrived, I asked to be seated outdoors. We had a very nice lunch and a glass of good wine, taking our time as we enjoyed the beautiful day together.

After lunch I suggested dessert, and Jenna did her "Oh no, don't tempt me honey" thing. She was okay with my ordering something, though, so we asked the waitress to bring the dessert tray.

The waitress presented the huge tray with a flourish. It was filled with a large variety of colorfully decorated pastries which I hoped Jenna would find irresistible, and she didn't disappoint me. The pretty little pastry in the middle called out to her just as I hoped it would.

Jenna reached out, pulled her hand back with a guilty look at me, then said, "Oh, what the heck! You only live once!" and picked up the pastry.

Rather than take a bite, though, she immediately began examining it more closely. "How funny. This is made just like a little box." She turned it from side to side and finally lifted the top of the pastry ever so slowly to see the diamond engagement ring I had bought her. Her face lit up like I'd never seen it before as she reached out to take my hand. "Yes! Yes! Yes!" she laughed.

Heck, I didn't even have to ask!

Tournament Prize

A professional golfer and his father were playing in a father/son golf tournament televised around the country. Caddying for the son was a beautiful young lady to whom he was planning a proposal of marriage.

The sportscasters announcing the tournament let the viewers in on what was about to happen. They watched avidly as she took the flag out of the hole and stood off to the edge of the green while the father putted out. As he reached in the hole to retrieve his ball, he secretly left a diamond ring in the bottom of the cup.

As the son's "caddy" looked down to replace the flag in the hole she saw the ring and jumped back in surprise. The young golfer walked over, retrieved the ring from the hole, and on his knee asked her to marry him.

Slipping the beautiful diamond ring on her finger, they embraced on the seventeenth green in front of a crowd of onlookers and golf fans watching all over the country.

What a Ride!

My girlfriend Emily and I had been dating for several years. We had both recently graduated from college and had embarked on our careers out in the "real world". A few weeks into our new jobs we were both feeling a little overwhelmed by reality, and I suggested that we do something out of the ordinary to lighten us up a bit. However, I had an ulterior motive that night . . .

We hopped in my car with no particular destination in mind, or so Emily thought, and headed toward the outskirts of town. The county fair was in full swing, and as we passed the fairgrounds, Emily turned to me and said, "I want to go ride the rides!" just like a little girl. That's one of the things I love about her so much, and just exactly what I had hoped would happen.

We paid our admission at the gate, and Emily immediately grabbed my hand and dragged me off to the Tilt-a-Whirl. She loves the "wild" rides and laughed and shrieked like a kid as we twirled around and around. As we staggered off, I told her that it was my turn to choose.

I'm a bit more on the tame side when it comes to carnival rides, so I suggested the ferris wheel. I have always loved the smooth, gliding circle that gives you a view of the whole carnival and the city beyond.

As Emily stepped in front of me to sit in the ferris wheel seat, I quickly turned to the operator, pointed straight up in the air and flashed him the diamond ring I was planning to present to Emily at the top of the ride. He got my drift and gave me a nod and a wink.

The ride slowed every few seconds as the operator let more passengers on, while Emily and I cuddled with contented smiles on our faces. Then we really got going. We went around and around quite a few times, until I was beginning to think the operator hadn't understood after all. Finally we gradually began to slow down until Emily and I surveyed the world from the top of the ferris wheel.

"Oh, honey, isn't this so romantic?" Emily exclaimed.

I looked at this beautiful woman with her childlike enthusiasm and felt my heart melt. I took her face in my hands and said, "Emily, do you have any idea how much I love you?"

She smiled up at me but knew there was no response needed.

I reached into my pocket and took her left hand in mine. "Emily, my love, will you be my wife?" I asked as I slid a diamond engagement ring on her finger.

As she leaned forward to hug me and say "Yes," the lights on the ferris wheel began to flash on and off wildly, and the carnival workers gathered below let out a big cheer.

Twelve years later, Emily and I (and the kids too!) still love to ride the ferris wheel and make it a point to share a ride whenever the carnival comes to town.

What's in the Box Honey?

Richard knew he'd need to enlist the help of his father-in-law-to-be in order to carry out his plan to present Mary with a diamond engagement ring. Richard and George discussed the role that each would play, and the plan was set in motion.

Richard had himself encased in a square wooden crate at George's carpentry shop. Small air holes were drilled in the side of the box so Richard could secretly look out without anyone else being able to see in.

After renting a questionable-looking old truck, Richard hired a couple of men to deliver the wooden crate laden with official stamps and addresses to Mary's home. Mary's father answered the door and signed for the box, yelling, "Mary, there's a box out here for you. What in the heck did you buy now?"

Everyone was saying, "What is it?" "Why don't you open it?" "Hurry up!" until finally George said, "Let me get a hammer and some tools, and let's see what's in here."

Excitement levels ran high, particularly for Mary, her mother, and her sister. They became increasingly frustrated with George as he took his own sweet time to open the box. He pried the lid open one nail at a time. Finally opened, he gently removed the lid and set it on the floor.

Mary looked in, and all she could see was a large circular disk which had written on it, "I love you . . . will you marry me?"

"What going on here?" she laughed, pulling on the circular, hat-like object. Up popped Richard with a big smile on his face. "Mary, you are the most beautiful, kind, caring person I've ever known, and I'd like to spend the rest of my life with you . . . will you marry me?"

With tears in her eyes, Mary whispered "Yes" as Richard slipped a diamond ring on her finger.

Warm Fuzzies

Our family celebrates Christmas with a vengeance . . . gifts overflowing beneath the tree like we're the richest people on earth. In abundance of love we are rich; in money we're not exactly drowning in it! But we enjoy a Christmas tradition of buying each other small, entertaining gifts throughout the year so we have lots of presents when we get home from church on Christmas morning.

David and I had been dating for almost two years, and I wanted him to share in all of our Christmas fun and blessings. I invited him to join my family for the holiday.

On Christmas morning we were having the time of our lives laughing and teasing each other about the outrageous gifts we had each received. David had even gotten his share of funny gifts and managed to sneak in a few of his own. He had given my Mom a potholder shaped like a pig and my Dad an apron saying "Kiss the Cook".

Everyone in the room burst out laughing when I opened the box he had wrapped so carefully to conceal a pair of bedroom slippers shaped like big elephant heads. "These are so adorable!" I said as I took my old slippers off to replace them with the new ones.

I pulled the first elephant head onto my right foot and waggled it at him with a big grin. Then I pulled the second slipper on, but "Ouch!" There was something stuck in there! I reached in to see what it was. As I pulled out a sparkling diamond engagement ring, David knelt down in front of me and took it from my hand.

As he held the ring poised at my finger, he said, "Denise, I can't think of a better time and place to ask you to be my wife. Will you marry me?"

David's beautiful surprise had left me speechless, but my family helped me out with shouts of "Say yes!"

"Of course I'll marry you David," I responded. "I'd be proud to be your wife."

What a wonderful Christmas memory that will always be for my whole family.

Abracadabra

Keith wasn't much for the big days like Valentine's Day, birthdays, and anniversaries, but Peggy loved special occasions and always managed to drop hints and reminders a week or two before so that Keith wouldn't forget.

At least Keith could always be counted on to make reservations at their favorite restaurant, and this year for their anniversary was no different. As they finished dressing for their evening out, Peggy handed Keith a box and said, "Honey, I think I finally found you the perfect gift."

Keith sheepishly unwrapped the box and opened it to reveal the neatest multi-function watch he had ever seen. Not only did it tell the time but it also gave the temperature, altitude, barometric pressure, had a directional compass, and had an alarm that could be set for everything imaginable.

Putting the watch on, Keith looked at Peggy and stammered, "Peg, honey, I um..."

"I know, honey" she said. "It's all right. I know you love me. Let's go to dinner."

After enjoying a superb meal, Keith ordered a bottle of champagne to celebrate their tenth anniversary. Just as they were being served the champagne, a wandering magician who had been working the tables throughout the restaurant appeared at their table and asked, "Would you like to see a great feat of magic?" to which they both answered "Yes."

With that, the magician picked up the champagne bottle and, holding it three feet above the glasses, proceeded to fill each glass without a single drop hitting the table. Then he said, "Before you drink, might I borrow that ring you have on your finger, sir?" gesturing to Keith's wedding band.

But when he tried to remove the ring, Keith found that it wouldn't budge. With a disappointed look on his face the magician turned to Peggy and said, "Ma'am, might I have that ring on your finger?" pointing to her diamond wedding ring.

Somewhat reluctantly Peggy took the ring off and handed it to him. Withdrawing a silk scarf from his pocket, the magician placed it over the ring in his hand and asked her if she would grab two ends of the scarf and gently pull it away from the ring.

Grabbing the scarf, Peggy did as she was instructed and was amazed to see that her ring had completely disappeared. In its place was a small black box. The magician said, "Ma'am, let me ask you a question . . . would you rather have the ring that was on your finger or take a chance on whatever's in this box?"

Peggy responded by saying, "Well, of course, I'd rather have my own ring back." To which the magician replied, "Certainly. I believe that's your ring in the bottom of your champagne glass." She looked and was shocked to see that it was.

"But," the magician said, "as a token of my appreciation for your time, I'd like you to have this box, too," and handed it to her as he backed away from the table to disappear into the next room.

Opening the box Peggy found an emerald cut diamond surrounded by several smaller diamonds. Keith took both of her hands and said, "Peg, ten years ago when I asked you to marry me I could only afford a very, very small diamond. I promised you that someday I would get you 'your' diamond . . . happy anniversary, darling."

She took the ring from the box, slid it on her finger, and with a brilliant smile thanked Keith for making this a magical anniversary memory that would last a lifetime.

Cat Fancy

Sharon and Keith had shared twenty-five years of marriage, and in that time Sharon had never asked for much, but Keith always knew she really wanted a pearl necklace.

Quietly slipping out of bed on the morning of their anniversary, he took the beautiful pearl necklace he had bought her and wrapped it around the neck of Shazzam, the family cat. Then he jumped back into bed and waited.

The alarm went off, and that was the signal for Shazzam to leap up onto the bed and remind his mistress by patting her gently on the cheek that it was time to get up.

Sharon woke slowly and with her eyes closed began to affectionately stroke the cat. She stopped at Shazzam's neck, and with her eyes still closed felt the pearl necklace carefully. She opened her eyes slowly to see if she was really touching what she thought she was touching, and as she laughed with delight over his wonderful surprise, her husband exclaimed, "Happy anniversary, honey . . . I love you!"

Golf Partners

Jean and Al played golf together every Sunday afternoon and today, their fifteenth wedding anniversary, was no different. They were very competitive, very evenly matched, but Al always managed to self destruct and bogie the last few holes. Jean always took advantage and won.

Playing in their favorite foursome, they had arrived at the eighteenth hole. Al said, "Once again you took advantage of me on the seventeenth hole." Dropping to his knees he continued, "And now I bow down and pay homage to you; here, I'll even tee up your ball for you."

After teeing up the ball he took his club, waved it over the ball saying a few magical words, drew a large three-foot circle around the ball on the tee, again saying some foolish incantation, then finally picked up some grass and dropped it on the ball. Bending over once again, he blew the grass from the ball and invited her to step to the tee.

Because Al was usually the more serious of the two, Jean didn't know whether to be amused or annoyed with him, but she certainly was confused. Taking her address, she swung, hit the ball, and watched in amazement as it exploded into a million pieces.

On the tee in front of where the ball had been was a little note which she picked up and read: "Why would anyone ever carry two 7-woods in their bag?" Indignantly she looked at Al and said, "I don't have two 7-woods!" She walked over to her bag to look and, sure enough, there were two 7-woods.

She pulled her own 7-wood out and then grabbed for the other one. Hearing a rattling noise, she slid her hand down the club shaft and stopped. Tied to the club with a red ribbon was a gorgeous cocktail ring, the one she had fallen in love with the last time she and Al had gone window shopping.

She turned to Al with a combined look of love and astonishment. He was beaming from ear to ear and said, "Happy anniversary, Jeanie. You've given me the best fifteen years of my life, and I'm looking forward to the next fifteen."

As they finished the hole, Al said, "I finally found what it takes to win the last hole in our golf game!"

Just Like a Little Boy

*F*rank's mother had always treated him with a great deal of love and attention. She faithfully attended all of his school events, never missed one of his baseball games, fixed him three healthy meals a day, and always emptied his pockets before putting his laundry into the washing machine.

Janet, Frank's wife of ten years, also loved to attend his "over-40" softball games and prepared sumptuous meals for him, but she put her foot down at emptying his pockets when doing the laundry — she had told him repeatedly that he was a grown man and could be responsible for that himself.

But after years of begging, pleading, and nagging she finally gave up. Now it was just another chore.

Saturday afternoon was laundry day, and as usual she shook her head in exasperation as she lifted Frank's trousers from the floor and felt the weight of the usual odds & ends he had the habit of collecting. But she was in a forgiving mood today. After all, it was their anniversary, and she knew he would take her out for a lovely celebration tonight.

"That man," she muttered, as she reached into his pants pocket to remove who knew what. This time, however, the offending item was not so much offending as intriguing . . . a long, narrow package wrapped in gold foil and topped with a mass of golden ribbons, almost too pretty to open.

Attached to the package was a note that read, "Honey, there have been two wonderful women in my life; I'm thankful that you're one of them. Thanks for taking such good care of me. I love you very much. Happy anniversary. Frank."

Anne turned and beamed with pleasure at Frank who was leaning in the laundry room doorway waiting for her to open her package. Inside was the most exquisite gold necklace Anne had ever seen. As she walked over to give Frank a thank-you kiss, she said, "Honey, I love you too, and I think I can even put up with emptying your pants pockets for another hundred years or so."

Mystery Box

Maria woke from a deep sleep with her daughter Jill shaking her and yelling, "Mommy! Mommy! There's a box hanging from the ceiling. What is it?"

She stumbled out of bed saying, "What are you talking about?" as she followed her daughter downstairs to the living room.

Sure enough, suspended from the ceiling was a mysterious-looking box. It was about eighteen inches square and wrapped in shiny tin foil. It looked like something from outer space!

"Don't . . . touch . . . the . . . box . . . !" They looked around at the sound of Dad's booming voice as he repeated, "Don't touch the box, please." By now Jill's two sisters had also come down to the living room, and Dad just looked at each of them, smiled, and said, "Don't touch the box."

Maria walked over to him with a quizzical look on her face and whispered, "Fred, what's going on? What's this box?" He just looked her in the eye and said, "Under no circumstances is anyone to touch that box."

One day passed, then another, then another until the box had been hanging from the ceiling in the living room for four days. Maria and the girls were going crazy wondering what was in it and, more importantly, who was it for? Deductive reasoning proved that no one's birthday was coming up; it certainly wasn't Valentine's Day or a wedding anniversary. Christmas was six months away. What could it be?

The excitement grew until finally, on the morning of the fifth day, Dad said, "I have an announcement to make . . . tonight someone in this room will open the box."

That evening with everyone gathered in the living room, Dad reached over, took the box in his hand and carefully cut the four wires that were holding it in suspension. He handed it to Jill, asking her to unwrap the tin foil from the box. When she had completed that, he took the box from her and handed it to his next oldest daughter, Rachel, and asked her to remove the box which was taped around yet another package.

The suspense continuing to build, Rachel unveiled a cylindrical object that Dad took from her and handed to his oldest daughter, Becky, asking her to open it.

Inside she revealed a small gift-wrapped package with a red velvet ribbon.

Fred picked up the box and handed it to Maria saying, "Happy anniversary, sweetheart."

"What are you talking about Fred?" she said. "This isn't our anniversary. Our anniversary isn't for three months!"

Fred walked over and put his arms around her, saying, "Actually dear, this IS our anniversary. Ten years ago today you walked into the little store where I was working. That's when I first saw you and that's when I first fell in love with you."

Grinning from ear to ear in surprise and pleasure, Maria opened the box to find a beautiful pair of star sapphire earrings.

Pearls of Wisdom

Celebrating fifteen years of marriage, Frank and Dede were finally on the dream vacation of a lifetime in Belize. It had been ten years since they'd been able to take a trip devoted to their passion for scuba diving, and they intended to spend as much time under water as possible for the next seven days.

As a dive master loaded equipment onto a boat for their much-anticipated first diving day, the sun was just coming up over the horizon. Frank and Dede sat on the top deck of the boat and sipped freshly squeezed, icy-cold orange juice as they watched the loading project. A charge of excitement shot through them as the boat slowly pulled away from the pier.

Today's dive would be at the old "pirate ship", at least that's what everyone called it. There were rumored to be great treasures of gold aboard this sailing vessel at one time. Only a few coins and some small trinkets had ever been salvaged.

After a thorough check of their equipment, Frank kicked his feet backwards, splashing into the water, followed by Dede. He took her hand as they slowly descended the short distance to the ship.

They swam around the old ship, peeked into some of the doors and windows, and examined some of the intricate woodwork which was in remarkable condition for such an old ship.

After lunch they were back in the water, this time exploring just at the bow of the old ship. Seeing Frank turning over rocks and scouring the bottom of the ocean floor, Dede began to do the same. After poking around under a variety of rocks and shipwreck debris, she picked up what looked like a small rock and then dropped it in surprise. She moved her hands frantically to get Frank's attention and motioned him over to see what she had found.

When Frank reached her, she pointed to the oyster at her feet. What excited Dede was the fact that not only was the oyster partially open, but coming from inside the oyster was not just one pearl — there appeared to be a whole string of pearls! Frank gestured for her to pick it back up, which she did, very carefully.

As she slowly pulled the string of pearls from their hiding place she turned to look at Frank and saw him mouthing the words, "I love you, honey. Happy anniversary!" They drifted slowly to the surface where she thanked him with a big kiss and a hug.

Who's That Knocking at My Door?

Joe traveled a great deal with his job but never failed to call Becky every evening when he was traveling. His phone call this night, however, couldn't make up for the fact that it was their wedding anniversary, and he wasn't there to celebrate it with her.

The phone rang and Becky picked it up, desperately trying not to let him hear in her voice how hurt she really was. For fifteen minutes they were laughing and joking and he was telling her his plan for how they would celebrate their anniversary as soon as he arrived home from his trip.

Their conversation was interrupted by a loud knocking on the front door. Becky figured it was probably her neighbor Cindy bringing goodies over to cheer her up.

Walking toward the front door with the phone up to her ear, still visiting with Joe, she swung the door open and almost passed right out!

There stood Joe, a cellular phone propped on his shoulder as he continued to speak to her, a bottle of champagne in his right hand, and a beautifully gift-wrapped box holding a diamond bracelet in his left. As he handed her the gift he said, "Our anniversary celebration begins right now. Happy anniversary, sweetheart. I love you."

The Christmas Sing

Christmas at our house was always a very festive time of the year, and finding just the right tree topped our list of importance when it came to decorating. Tree hunting was a family affair that included my dad, my mother, my little sister, and me. It always seemed like we had to visit every tree lot in town before we found the perfect tree. But, once we were gathered around our specially-picked tree that we had decorated "just so", we were very pleased with our efforts.

Another of our family traditions was to gather around the piano on Christmas Eve and sing Christmas carols. This Christmas was no different . . . with Mom playing the piano, we began working our way through the Christmas carol book, each of us choosing a favorite. As we concluded every song, Mom would tap repeatedly on the middle C saying, "This just doesn't sound right." Not being pianists, we all kind of shrugged our shoulders and went on to the next song.

Finally, after a half dozen songs, she'd had it. Standing up, she said, "There really is something wrong with this key!" and asked my father to lift the lid of the piano so she could see why the key wasn't hitting right.

As Mom looked down into the piano, she exclaimed, "Well, no wonder! There's something stuck on one of the wires." She reached in to remove it and further exclaimed, "Somebody taped something on here . . . what's going on?"

Mom fiddled with the tape for a few seconds and popped up with a beautiful emerald stud earring held up for inspection between her thumb and forefinger. She turned around to see all of us with these lovingly goofy grins on our faces as my father held out the box containing the other earring. "Merry Christmas, honey, from all of us."

Too Old for Dolls

Several years ago when Cabbage Patch dolls were all the rage and almost impossible to get, my mother, who was in her late fifties then, was adamant that one of those dolls was the only thing she really wanted for Christmas. My father, who always did his best to give Mom anything she wanted, launched a diligent search until he finally found one — the cost was something he never disclosed.

Christmas Day came and our whole family waited in anticipation to see Mom's reaction when she saw that Dad had actually found her a Cabbage Patch doll. We hovered close as Dad sat smugly watching in the background. Mom slowly unwrapped the package and exclaimed with pure pleasure when she saw the funny-looking little doll peeking out at her.

Pulling the doll from its box, Mom gave it a hug and then held her out at arm's length for further inspection. Suddenly, she pulled the doll back close to her face very quickly and then looked up at my father with such a look of surprise we couldn't figure out what was going on! "Let us see, Mom," we all begged.

She turned the doll slowly around, the whole time looking at my father with tears in her eyes, and there around the doll's neck was a spectacular diamond necklace, the likes of which I don't think Mom ever thought she would own.

Fifteen years later, my mother wears that necklace every single day. . . and at night it rests around the little Cabbage Patch doll's neck.

Udderly Surprised

My husband Richard and I always go back to the Midwest for Christmas knowing full well that even though we complain about the snow and cold, it's really the best part of our whole year. Helping with the chores, cooking in the big farm kitchen, and sitting peacefully around the Christmas tree all help remind us that there's a simpler world to live in.

As much as I hated doing chores when I was a little girl, I look forward to those early morning trips to the barn to feed the hogs and milk the two cows my mom insists be kept so as to always have fresh milk and cream. Mmmmm, nothing like fresh cream in your coffee — real cream! And a hot cinnamon roll fresh out of the oven. Both would be waiting for us when we finished seeing to it that all of the animals were fed and watered.

It's no different on Christmas morning. We all trudge out to the barn, kids included, and we grumble and moan about having to take time away from the cozy fire and stack of unopened gifts.

This Christmas morning I volunteered to do the milking because I'm not all that fond of starting my day greeted by a bunch of pigs. The kids ran off to gather fresh eggs for breakfast, and I pulled up a stool and got down to business.

As I listened to the music of Moo's milk hitting the bucket, I kept noticing that Big Mama standing next to us was awfully restless. "Take it easy Big Mama. I'm going as fast as I can here. What are you so antsy about anyway?" I kept up my chatter hoping to calm Big Mama enough to finish up with Moo.

Big Mama was not to be calmed though. "Hold that thought Moo," I said as I got up to check Mama and make sure nothing was wrong.

I patted Big Mama on the head and started to check her out to make sure everything was okay. She just seemed a little skittish, not sick in any way. I ran my hand across her back and down her flank. Everything fine there. Then I knelt down beside her to make sure she didn't have some sort of inflammation of her udders.

That's when I burst out laughing and reached out to remove the loosely tied ribbon that held a tiny little foil-wrapped package swinging in the air. "Richard, you goofball, you're making Big Mama a nervous wreck!" I laughed as he walked over to pat Mama on the side, shushing to calm her down.

Inside the box was a beautiful pair of ruby earrings that I will always cherish. Not only do they remind me of how much Richard loves me, but they also remind me of the good times on the farm at Christmas.

Why Not a Blender?

Shelly knew Christmas wasn't a big time of the year for Sam. He dutifully cut down a tree, strung the lights, and even hung a few ornaments, but he never really seemed to get into the "spirit" of the season.

On Christmas morning, Sam sipped his coffee and watched patiently as the kids tore into their gifts with great enthusiasm, "oohing" and "aahing" over all the fun stuff. Shelly took great pleasure from unwrapping each of her packages precisely as she prolonged the enjoyment of each gift. There was a nice blouse from her mom, a very pretty outfit from Sam (which she had picked out herself), some cute handmade gifts from the kids, and various odds & ends from her friends and family.

Sam quietly enjoyed opening his gifts but was more interested in watching everyone else. When it seemed as though there were no more gifts under the tree, Sam reached way back and handed Shelly one last package. It was heavy, too heavy to be those earrings to match the necklace he'd surprised her with eons ago. Unwrapping the box, she pulled out, of all things, a blender.

Well, after all, he was a practical man. He did love her, and this showed it . . . she guessed. "Open it," he said, "this is the best one on the market."

Opening the box, she pulled the blender out and saw that it contained a lavishly gift-wrapped little box, and she began to feel butterflies in her stomach. She reached down in and pulled the box out. When she opened it, she found her matching pair of diamond earrings. Tears welled up in her eyes as she looked at Sam. He matched her teary gaze as he said, "Honey, I love you. Merry Christmas."

A Roll of the Dice

Birthdays at our house were always very special — my father made sure of it. He always had some crazy game he had dreamed up for us to play as we "searched" for our gift.

To celebrate my mother's birthday one year, my father assembled us all in the family room. He produced a one-foot-square pillow (dice) and about twenty cards which he spread in a meandering line on the floor, each card about 18 inches from the next, similar to a pathway in which one might move their "piece" on a game board.

The object . . . roll the dice, pace off the appropriate number, reach down and pick up a card, read aloud what it said, and then follow the directions to the best of your ability. Mom rolled the dice for a four, paced off four cards on the floor, picked up the fourth card which read: "Tennis anyone? Receive one dollar for every time you are able to bounce a ball up in the air off a tennis racket . . . sitting down."

Ever tried to bounce a ball on a tennis racket while sitting down? Practically impossible but great fun to watch! Mom earned about three dollars on that one.

She continued to roll the dice, step off the cards, pick them up, read them, and even made a few dollars. Some of the tasks were extremely inventive: "Call the dog. If she comes on the first call, win $10; the second call, win $5; the third call 50 cents. How many glasses is the dishwasher designed to accommodate? How many steps on the stairway to the second floor? How many shoe boxes in your closet?" Money was rewarded on a sliding scale based on how close Mom was to the correct number.

When Mom got to the last card, it read: "Go to your room!" We all looked at each other and then raced up to the master bedroom. Upon entering we saw the glow of two candles, a beautiful red rose on my mother's pillow, and next to the rose a box Mom opened to find a pair of beautiful emerald earrings.

My father took my mother's hand and said, "Honey, you are the greatest treasure in my life. I rolled the dice thirteen years ago, and I've been a winner ever since. Happy birthday."

Closet Surprise

Today was Susan's birthday, and she hummed happily as she drove home from work. She was really looking forward to dinner at her favorite restaurant with her husband Paul. A neighbor had agreed to take care of the kids for the evening, and Susan had nothing to do but get ready and have a fun evening.

The telephone was ringing as she walked in the front door, and she rushed to answer it. It was Paul, and he didn't even tell her happy birthday. He just announced that his boss had assigned him an urgent project that needed to be completed by eight o'clock the following morning. He followed up by saying that in the bedroom closet he had a briefcase full of documents he needed immediately to do the project. His request, "Would you please do me a big favor and bring those to me at the office?" added to the disappointment that was now beginning to set in. The evening she had looked forward to was not going to happen, and he hadn't even mentioned her birthday.

Paul explained where the briefcase was in the closet and said he'd wait on the phone while she went to find it.

Susan went to the bedroom closet and flipped the light switch . . . nothing happened. "Great," she muttered, "what else can go wrong?" She moved cautiously into the closet, certain she knew where the briefcase was. She stopped short when suddenly a match was struck and she saw a candle being lit, then another candle, then another. She watched in surprise as candle by candle a birthday cake was illuminated by her husband, who was sitting on the floor with the cake on a small table in front of him. He was wearing a party hat and began singing "Happy Birthday" as he continued to light candles.

This was too funny! Paul was the most serious, business-like person in the world. And there he sat on the closet floor wearing a goofy hat and singing happy birthday. Susan couldn't believe it!

Paul invited her to sit on the floor across from him at the little table. "Honey, make a wish and blow out the candles." She did as he instructed but had some difficulty because his surprise appearance had left her a bit giggly. The next thing she heard was a distinct "pop," and Paul was pouring champagne into two glasses.

Touching his glass to hers, Paul became his serious self again and said, "Susan, you're the love of my life. I love you with all my heart, and I am so thankful that you're my wife. Happy birthday." He opened a pretty little velvet-covered box to reveal a wonderful opal ring glittering in the candlelight.

With tears in both of their eyes, he carefully slipped it on her finger.

Hamburgers Your Way

"Where should we go for dinner tonight?" Dad asked. "McDonald's!" my sister and I yelled in unison.

"Okay. Let's go," said Dad, and the four of us, Dad, Mom, my sister and I, jumped in the car and took off for McDonald's.

Mom's birthday was three days away, but Dad had already rigged a surprise for her. Unknown to any of us, he had already visited McDonald's earlier in the day in order to set up the surprise.

Working with the McDonald's assistant manager, they carefully hollowed out a large hamburger bun which would fit a tiny box containing a gift Mom had always wanted. The "burger" was then wrapped up in its normal foil covering, and the employees were all alerted to the signal which Dad would give at the drive-through.

The plan was that we would drive up to the window, Dad would place the order, and our hamburgers and fries would be placed in a bag along with the "gift burger." All Dad had to do to get the plan rolling was ask us the question, "Where do you want to go for dinner?" because he knew what our answer would be, since McDonald's is always our answer!

So now we drove to McDonald's. Dad placed the order and gave the signal by asking for lots of extra mustard and ketchup. We picked it up at the window and were on our way to our favorite picnic table in the park three blocks away.

Sitting at the table, Dad passed our food out to each of us. Mom unwrapped her hamburger, then held it out at arm's length, looking at it very suspiciously. She's been caught up in my father's practical jokes on more than one occasion, and this was beginning to look a little fishy.

Suddenly she exclaimed, "What kind of a hamburger did you order for me anyway? What is this?" As she lifted the top of the bun she saw a colorfully wrapped gift box tucked inside. By now my sister and I had stopped eating and were watching the proceedings carefully. My father looked on, beaming with pleasure at yet another well-executed plan.

Mom opened the box to find a wonderful pair of pearl earrings as Dad leaned over to give her a kiss on the cheek. "I love you, Jeannie. Happy birthday."

But that wasn't all. My father reached into his pocket and produced two small gift-wrapped boxes and handed them to my sister and me as he said, "The two of you are also very special to me." Inside each box was a little heart-shaped locket with our initials on it.

That day is one memory of growing up that I truly cherish.

Let's Make a Deal

No matter what her age, Patricia's birthday was always a big deal. It was her special day, and she loved to make the most of it. Dave decided to involve the couple's two young daughters in a birthday game for Patricia where the ultimate prize was . . . well, something very nice.

Fashioned after the television game show, "Let's Make A Deal", Dave gave his wife Patricia 20 one dollar bills to start the game.

Approaching a chest with three drawers, Dave said, "You may pick drawer number one, drawer number two, or drawer number three . . . in one drawer is a fifty dollar bill, in another is a five dollar bill, and in the third drawer there's nothing. For five dollars, which drawer do you choose?"

Patricia handed over five one dollar bills. The girls were jumping up and down and shouting, "Choose number one Mommy!" "No, choose number two Mommy!" "No, choose number three!" Finally she selected drawer number two, and in it was a fifty dollar bill. She and the girls jumped up and down with excitement.

Dave said, "Had you chosen drawer number one, you would have received five dollars," as he removed the five dollar bill. "And in drawer number three was a complete zilch — nothing!"

Walking into the kitchen, Dave said, "Here we have the dog's dish, and two cat dishes, one for each cat. For five of your one dollar bills, under one of those dishes is a fifty dollar bill, under the other is a five dollar bill, and under the third there is nothing . . . which do you choose?" Now the kids were really into it, first pointing to one dish and then another. Patricia pondered for some time before she made her decision.

After much deliberation, she chose the dog's dish, carefully lifted it, and under it, zilch. . . nothing! "Had you chosen this cat dish, you would have received fifty dollars, or under this dish," as he overturned it, "you would have found five dollars."

The game went on and on, some she won, some she lost, and some she broke even, but the excitement in the air was electric.

They ended up in the master bedroom staring at three pillows on the bed.

"Under one pillow is fifty dollars, under a second pillow five dollars, and under the third is nothing. Hand me five one dollar bills, and you can choose." Of course, the debate between the three ladies was once again very fervent.

Then Dave said, "Your head lies on one of the pillows as we sleep. My head lies on another pillow as we sleep. But the one in the middle . . . that's the one your daughters lie on when they come to sleep in our bed."

Patricia reached over and lifted the pillow in the middle; under it was a beautifully wrapped package. Inside she found the most exquisite sapphire ring she had ever seen with a note that read, "Happy birthday from three people who would not be here without you."

Scavenger Hunt

My husband Jim gets quite a kick out of himself and particularly enjoys creating ways to make gift-giving occasions special in his own quirky way. My favorite was the year we celebrated my birthday with a group of friends, and he organized a scavenger hunt. I hadn't done that in years!

My team and I started off on our search for the silly items on our list, determined to find one of each and be the big winners. More than likely our prize would be last year's leftover Halloween candy, but it was the principle of the thing!

We stopped first at my dear friend Molly's, an elderly woman who seldom left her home. I was certain she'd have at least a few of the things we needed. She didn't mind a bit when we borrowed a roll of toilet tissue, a salt shaker, a magazine, and some soda crackers. She was a gold mine!

Our next stop netted us a candy bar, some wrapping paper and ribbon, and a comb. And so the hunt went. We had twenty items to gather and could get a maximum of four from any one house. The more obscure items, like a cigarette holder and an aluminum can masher, had us searching for quite a while, but finally we had everything on the list.

When we arrived back at the house, we found that everyone else had finished ahead of us, but none of them had found everything on the list like we had. We were the big winners! Just as I had suspected, our prize was a silly one — a package of licorice for each of us!

As Jim rooted through our loot to make sure we hadn't cheated, he held up the salt shaker we had borrowed from Molly. "Come here honey. Doesn't this look a little strange?"

I walked over to see what he was talking about, and, yes, there was something other than salt in that shaker. Our curiosity got the best of us, so I went and got a bowl to empty the salt into.

Jim slowly poured as we all gathered around to see what was going to fall out. "Clink" we heard as something shiny hit the side of the bowl. "Oh my gosh! It's a gorgeous diamond earring!" I exclaimed. The matching earring followed, and I said, "What on earth would Molly be doing with diamond earrings in her salt shaker?"

"You silly goose!" Molly said from the behind our guests. "Those earrings are from Jim, and he conned me into helping him get them to you in his usual outrageous fashion. I just think he's the sweetest man!"

I turned to Jim, "I think he's the sweetest man too! Thanks honey! This is your best surprise ever!"

Surprise Party

*I*t was Mom's thirtieth birthday, and Dad wanted to have a surprise party for her. Rather than take Mom out of the house and bring her back to a house full of friends, he tried the ultimate challenge . . . to sneak thirty people into the house while she was there!

He let us in on what was going to happen, but he was a bit concerned that my ten-year-old younger sister's excitement would cause Mom to be suspicious.

First he had to get the house clean. There, of course, was no way HE could do it because that would be a big clue that something was going on. So he told Mom he had invited his boss and his wife over for a game of bridge, and they would be bringing their two-year-old son. This accomplished two things. Number one, it gave my mother a reason to tidy up the house, and since my sister loved to take care of their little boy, the ploy would disguise her excitement over the surprise party.

Dad arranged for everyone to gather at the neighbor's house immediately across the street. They were to call the house when everyone was assembled.

The telephone rang, Dad answered it, and said, "Okay . . . we'll see you when you get here," and then told Mom that our bridge guests would be a little late.

Then the action began: Dad called for Mom to help him search for a contact lens he had allegedly lost in the upstairs bathroom. As they were on the floor searching for the contact lens, thirty people were sneaking into the lower family room. That was my signal to come running upstairs yelling, "Mom! Mom! Susan is sick! She's throwing up!" At that very moment Dad miraculously found his contact lens. Mom grabbed some towels and then came tearing down the stairs to the family room to be greeted by a big "SURPRISE!" from all of her friends.

She practically fell down the last few stairs she was so shocked! She turned around and there was Dad standing behind her. He placed a beautiful box in her hand, saying, "Happy birthday, honey, and I look forward to the next thirty years!"

Mom opened the box to find a breathtaking diamond pendant. As tears streamed down her face, Dad took the necklace from her hands and fastened it around her neck. He gave her a big kiss and then declared, "Party time!"

The Shape You're In

Except for the fact that it was my fortieth birthday, this was just like any other Tuesday for me. Get up, fix breakfast for the kids, help Toby get his track gear ready, fix Mary a sack lunch, and then off to the gym for a workout.

As usual, my husband Chuck was up and gone early, grabbing coffee and a bagel on his way to work. "I wish that man could get his mind off of work for just two minutes," I muttered as I jogged on the treadmill. It would have been nice if he had rolled over this morning and at least said "happy birthday" or, even better, had made me breakfast in bed. That was a lot to wish for, but it sure would have been nice.

As I picked up my pace on the treadmill, I considered ways to get Chuck to join me at the gym. The last gym Chuck had ever seen was the one in the jungle — as in jungle gym at his grade school playground. No matter how much I tell him that I worry about him working so much and that he isn't taking very good care of himself physically, he just ignores my pleas.

"Oh well, enough of that," I told myself, looking around to see the usual familiar faces. As I finished up with my run and stepped down, my girlfriend Julie walked over and said, "Marge, I'm having trouble getting this weight adjusted over here. Could you give me a hand for just a second?"

I said I would and we both walked over to the abdominal "cruncher". I have to admit that I was subconsciously aware of a larger than normal group of people sort of milling around in the area, but it didn't really sink in since we were chatting about the new aerobics instructor.

All of a sudden, a loud chorus of "Happy Birthday" broke out. When I realized that everyone in the gym was singing to me, I just couldn't believe. I hadn't told a soul it was my birthday, so who leaked it?

Then I got my answer. There stood Chuck right in the middle of the group singing "Happy Birthday", and I was even more shocked to see that he was wearing workout clothes. Wow! What a wonderful birthday gift! He walked over and gave me a big hug.

"Honey, I've finally decided to give in to your coaxing to start working out with you. That's one of your birthday presents. The other is in this box," he said as he held out a box gift-wrapped in shiny gold paper.

Opening the box with shaky hands, I found a stunning watch inscribed with the words, "Time together well spent . . . Love, Chuck." Two wonderful birthday gifts made my fortieth birthday an especially happy one.

Treasure Hunt

My husband Tom and I always treated our sons to a treasure hunt on Christmas morning so they would truly be surprised by gifts that were impossible to disguise with wrapping paper. One year they found a computer at the end of the hunt; another year they found bowling balls. It was a game that brought all of us a great deal of pleasure.

On my birthday this year, I came home from work to find a note pinned to the front door; it read: "Dear birthday girl, go back into the garage and see if there's anything of interest to you in the tool box. Love, Tom."

I returned to the garage and eagerly opened the tool box to find another note: "It's a day off from cooking for you, but you still might want to check out the cookware under the oven to make sure it's in good shape." Hmmm, good shape?

I went into the kitchen, straight to the oven, and opened the drawer beneath it. Inside it was the cookware just like I'd been coveting at my sister's house for months. What a terrific birthday gift! But, no, there was another note there: "Don't stop here. I know you're dying to get those heels off and get into something comfy for your special birthday evening."

Off to the bedroom I went, and there I found a beautifully set table with flowers and the good china. On the bed was a pretty little summery dress that I could slip on and be comfortable in yet look good at the same time! Boy, does that husband of mine have great taste!

I picked up the dress and another note fell out: "Put on your new dress, pour yourself a glass of wine, and I'll be home in a few minutes."

I changed into my dress, sat down at the pretty table, and poured myself a glass of wine from the bottle in the ice bucket that had miraculously appeared while I was in the closet. Suddenly soft music began playing and Jim appeared in the doorway with a satisfied grin on his face. "Are you enjoying this so far honey?" he asked.

"Of course I am! I love my gifts!" I told him.

"Well, here's another direction for your treasure hunt," he said as he handed me one last note: "Go into the closet and look in the pocket."

"What pocket?" I thought. But I went in and began feeling around in every suit, jacket, and coat pocket I could find. I hit the jackpot when I stuck my hand in the pocket of my winter coat. Something long and narrow and bumpy — it felt like a bracelet of some sort. I savored the moment as I tried to figure out exactly what it was, then pulled out a breathtaking diamond bracelet! I can't even begin to say how surprised I was — it was the last thing on earth I would have expected!

As I turned to hug Tom and tell him thank you he said, "Happy birthday, honey! You're very special to me, and I wanted to show you that in a special way."

Be My Valentine

*D*uring the month of February, we men start to get nervous. There are expectations out there that we're just not sure we're equipped to handle. The Valentine's Day thing is a bit scary!

My wife Sara starts dropping little hints in late January that she really enjoyed last year when I bought her the dozen roses or the special dinner out that we did the year before. I start thinking, "How do I top myself year after year?" But never fear, the romantic side of me usually wins out, and this year was no exception.

On February 14th I gave her a quick peck on the cheek as I left for work, letting her think I hadn't remembered that it was Valentine's Day, then I high-tailed it out to the garage knowing she would be leaving shortly behind me.

I drove down the street and parked my car around the corner then snuck back to watch the show. I waved to my neighbor Tom as I crept around the side of his house, and he just shook his head.

I waited right outside the garage to hear the door from the house into the garage close, then I peeked cautiously around the corner.

Sara was preoccupied and looked at her watch as she opened the door to her little car. Whoosh! Out came the helium balloons I had so carefully crammed in there after she went to sleep last night.

She jumped back, startled, then looked around to see if I was hiding anywhere nearby. "I know you're out there somewhere Tim! What are you up to?"

As I came out from my hiding place I pointed to the front seat of the car where one last balloon rested. "I wonder why that one didn't fly out," I said. "Better check it out."

Sara reached in and pulled the balloon out of the car, shaking it to hear the rattle inside. I handed her the pin I had put on the shelf by the car and suggested she pop the balloon to get her real Valentine's Day surprise.

POP! went the balloon and out dropped a red velvet jewelry box that I caught in mid air and presented to Sara with a bow. "Honey, you are my sweetheart, forever and ever. Happy Valentine's Day."

The star sapphire earrings inside glistened like the tears in her eyes as she hugged me and said, "I love you Tim. You never disappoint me on Valentine's Day."

It's a Dog's World

My husband Kelly and I have a German Shepherd who seems to believe that if he's not barking, no one's giving him the attention he deserves. Sometimes I can actually identify with that, but for the most part I find it very aggravating — and so do the neighbors!

Our new neighbor, Bob, had made repeated visits to our home asking us very nicely to please do something about Buddy's barking. We tried everything we could think of short of putting a muzzle on him. Conversations with Bob gradually became less cordial over a period of just a few days, and I was feeling terribly stressed about the situation.

On Valentine's Day, a day when I should have been expecting a knock on the door from a delivery man bringing roses, I cringed when I heard the doorbell ring. Buddy had been barking frantically, and I had banished him to the back yard so I could get a few minutes of peace.

I took my time going to the door, hoping that I'd either find a nice gift waiting, or if it was Bob he would give up and go back home. No such luck on either score.

There stood Bob with an angry scowl on his face. "Susan! I've really had enough of that dog. I don't want to have a feud over this, but I sure would appreciate it if you would try this muzzle and see if it tones Buddy's barking down a little bit." At that, he held out a muzzle and I took it from him.

"Okay Bob," I replied quietly as I turned and walked back into the house. I really hated to do that to Buddy, but if that was the only answer, then so be it. I walked out the back door and knelt down beside Buddy to slip the muzzle over his nose.

As I looked down at the muzzle, however, I saw that there was something stuck inside it that would make it impossible to put on. I pulled out a small gift box wrapped in Valentine's Day paper and with even more curiosity than excitement I opened it to find the diamond teardrop earrings I'd been hinting to Kelly about for two years.

I ran back through the house and out the front door to find both Bob and Kelly waiting with expectant grins on their faces. "You guys set me up!" I laughed.

Kelly reached out and pulled me close in a hug. "Honey, Bob isn't even all that mad about Buddy. He's just been putting on a show the past few days. I wanted these earrings to be a real surprise when I gave them to you, and I think I succeeded, don't you?"

"Did you ever. And I love you for it!" I replied as I hugged him back.

Valentine's Day Scrooge

I had always been frustrated with my husband's lack of enthusiasm for Valentine's Day, meaning a card given halfheartedly was the most I could expect. But since he was a wonderful, loving husband and father and did nice things for me all year, I really couldn't complain.

However, on Valentine's Day, as my co-workers received flowers, candy, and romantic cards from their husbands and boyfriends, I couldn't help but feel sorry for myself.

Sue just got flowers . . . Becky just got a balloon bouquet . . . oooh, and a candy bouquet for Sara! I decided to take a quick break and go for a walk to blow off a little steam. It was near lunchtime; maybe I'd treat myself to a special Valentine's Day lunch.

As I walked out the door of my office building, I was approached by a mime. I had seen him "working the street" the past few weeks and got a kick out of his silent antics. Today he seemed to sense my blue mood and walked right up to me.

The mime drew his face into a sad one to match my expression and proceeded to entertain me with a series of scenarios that depicted sadness turned to happiness. At the end of his routine, he magically whipped out a bouquet of brightly-colored paper flowers and handed them to me with a flourish.

As I reached out to take them, he grasped my hand and opened it, palm flat. He took the flowers, gave them a little shake above my hand, and out dropped a ring. Thinking this was a continuation of his entertainment, I picked it up to examine it, and found it to be a curiously real-looking opal surrounded by tiny diamonds. This guy must be getting some great tips!

A hand reached out and touched my arm, and there stood my husband, Richard, smiling with the pleasure of a small child. "Honey," he said, "that ring is for you. Happy Valentine's Day. I love you."

"But, Richard, you don't believe in Valentine's Day!" I squeaked as I put the ring on and held it out in the sunlight to admire it.

"No, honey, that's not really true. I've just been saving up for something really special!"

Valentine's Day Surprise

I've been married to Jake for seventeen years now and have been one of those lucky women married to a thoughtful man who always makes Valentine's Day special. A romantic dinner at our favorite restaurant and a bouquet of gladiolas delivered to me at my office are the standard.

When Valentine's Day arrived last year with no bouquet of flowers and no mention of dinner, I wasn't just hurt, I was worried! What was wrong with our marriage? Or with me? Or with Jake? By the end of the day I couldn't wait to get home and find out what was going on!

I left my office in a rush, pulling on my jacket as I walked out the front door. Head down to search for my car keys, I ran straight into the driver who was waiting to escort me to the limousine idling at the curb. He opened the door and guided me gently toward the outstretched hand of my husband Jake.

He settled me into the seat across from him and handed me a glass of champagne. A scrumptious array of hors d' oeuvres sat on a candlelit counter to the side of us, and my bouquet of gladiolas served as decoration.

For a change I was speechless as Jake took my hand in his and held it in his warm embrace. "Honey, I thought after seventeen years of celebrating Valentine's Day in exactly the same way it was time for a change. I hope you don't mind."

"I have just one other addition, and then we'll enjoy our hors d' oeuvres and champagne on the way to dinner."

At that he reached down to the seat beside him and retrieved a red velvet jewelry case. Opening it very slowly, he revealed a necklace of diamonds that sparkled in the candlelight like a sky full of glittering stars. It literally took my breath away!

As Jake leaned over and fastened the necklace around my neck and touched his lips to mine, he whispered, "I love you honey. Happy Valentine's Day."

Monster Truck Mama!

*F*or the most part, my husband and kids treat me like a queen on Mother's Day. Last year, though, I was beginning to wonder if they had totally forgotten the day because all I was hearing about was that they had tickets to go to some big monster truck rally coming to town on "my" day! I kept trying to subtly remind them that there was a big day involved, and all I got was, "Yeah! Wow! This is going to be so cool!" So, finally, I decided that if I couldn't sway them in my direction I'd just have to join them at the rally and consider it a treat of a different sort!

Quite honestly, I had a terrific time at that truck rally. The roaring trucks doing unimaginable tricks, the speedsters who blew past us in a plume of smoke and flames . . . all of it was pretty exciting. I was getting into it so much that when my husband asked us if we'd like to go behind the grandstand and look at some of the trucks parked out there, I was the one saying, "Yeah! Cool! Let's check these things out up close!" He just grinned and shook his head at me.

The kids and I held each other's hands and trailed David out to the area where the trucks were parked, "oohing" and "aahing" at the size of those things. We stopped at a big purple truck that had tires as big as my whole car. I was fascinated with its sheer size, and when David asked me if I'd like to get inside it, my answer was an unhesitating "Yes!" He asked the owner if that would be okay, and between him and David they hoisted me up until I was sitting on top of the world surveying my kingdom from a monster truck.

I put my hands on the wheel, not quite doing a "vroom, vroom", but close. I felt like a kid playing grownup, and I decided at that moment that this really was a terrific Mother's Day.

I looked down at the dash to see what kind of gizmos would be included in such a truck and saw that an envelope was blocking my view. And the envelope had my name on it. I looked down at David and the kids to see them watching me avidly with huge grins on their faces. I picked up the envelope to find a small jewelry box sitting behind it but prolonged the moment by politely reading the very beautiful, loving card first. Then I picked up the pretty little box and removed the shimmering ribbons and gold paper. Inside was a pair of blue topaz earrings which I immediately put on and surveyed in the monster truck's rear view mirror to admire my family's good taste.

Climbing down to thank David and the kids, I realized that this truly had been a wonderful Mother's Day with my family, and I wouldn't have traded it for my "normal" Mother's Day for anything!

Whose Day Is This Anyhow?

I will never forget my first Mother's Day . . . breakfast in bed complete with a rose in a bud vase, waited on hand and foot all day, dinner out . . . you name it, I had it. Now that's what Mother's Day is all about, right? Wrong! That lasted about two years, and then our lives became so bogged down with everyday responsibilities I just never felt I could take a whole day to be pampered. Maybe breakfast in bed would be squeezed in, but that lasted about fifteen minutes and was accompanied by kids and dogs, all anxious to take advantage of my perceived "trapped" state tucked under the covers with a tray precariously balanced on my lap.

Two years ago, twelve years into motherhood, I had just made the usual calls to both my mom and my husband's mother to wish them happy Mother's Day when the doorbell rang. I had no idea how much I had missed the big "to-do" of my own Mother's Day until the moment I saw my husband standing at the door dressed as a delivery man and holding out an arrangement of irises. "Delivery for Mrs. Stone," he said quite formally.

I reached out to take the flowers with what I'm sure can only be described as a look of shock. "Thank you young man," I replied as I accepted them. "Would you like to come in for a cup of coffee? I'm afraid I don't have any change for a tip."

"Why, yes, thank you ma'am. I'd like that very much. Delivering flowers is much harder than most people realize you know." Ronnie joined me in the living room as I sat the flowers on the coffee table and went to get us each a cup of coffee. When I returned, he had removed his delivery man's cap and was gently rearranging the flowers, all three of the kids watching on with happy grins.

"Why, look here! There's something stuck down in these flowers!" he exclaimed as though surprised. At that, he dropped all pretenses and extracted a small golden box and held it in his hand, saying, "Janice, I'm afraid I'm very guilty of getting so wrapped up in everyday things that I don't take the time to tell you what a terrific wife and mother you are. Mother's Day slides by with barely an acknowledgement, but today I'm going to take advantage of the occasion to show you my appreciation." He was joined by a chorus of enthusiastic "Happy Mother's Day, Mommy. We love you!" from the kids.

I watched as he opened the lid of the box and removed a mother's ring with birthstones for each of our children and slid it on my right ring finger. "Thank you, sweetheart, for all that you do. I apologize for not saying it often enough, but it's always something I'm aware of. I love you very much."

After years of Mother's Day being just another day, my wonderful husband and children had just turned it into one of the most special days of my life.

Baby Talk

*T*he day my daughter Amber was born seventeen years ago was a proud and happy moment for Jimmy and me. Like all new parents, we were so proud we could burst, and Jimmy hovered anxiously over my bed all that first day as I held Amber in my arms.

Unlike today when a mother and child are typically out of the hospital in twenty-four to forty-eight hours, Amber and I spent four days there before being discharged. Jimmy spent as much time with us as he possibly could.

Every morning Jimmy teased me about my thorough examination of Amber as though I thought they would bring her to me some morning with parts missing — hands, arms, fingers, toes all present and accounted for. But on our last morning in the hospital, as I performed my daily inspection, I was shocked to find a little envelope tucked into the front of Amber's diaper. What on earth were these people doing?

I gently slid the envelope out of her diaper, finding that rather than paper, the envelope was made of the softest satin. I carefully opened the envelope to find a note that read, "Look in the bottom drawer of your nightstand." I handed Amber to Jimmy, who was looking on intently, and climbed out of bed to look in the nightstand.

There I found another note which read:

Our lives have changed forever

From now on it will only get better and better

To remind you of this precious time

A special gift is yours to find

At the bottom of the poem it read, "When you're finished with this note, ring for the charge nurse."

I pushed the button and almost immediately the nurse walked in with her little pill tray in hand and handed it to me with a smile. There was the familiar assortment of pills, but in the center was a little box wrapped in pink paper with a shimmering silver bow on top. "What's this?" I asked, to which the nurse just shrugged her shoulders.

I unwrapped the box and found a pair of tiny eighteen-carat gold baby booties. Just then Jimmy held out a beautiful gold charm bracelet. "This is a very special occasion in our lives, the birth of our first daughter. Every year on Amber's birthday we'll add another gold charm significant of her life at that moment. I love you, Deb." And then he held both Amber and me close in his big warm hug.

Happy New Year

*I*t was New Year's Eve, the dawning of the new year, and here they were getting ready to crawl into bed at ten o'clock just like any other night of the year. No amount of coaxing could convince Derrick to stay up to celebrate. "We can celebrate tomorrow," he said, and Anne, though she was a bit miffed, decided that celebrating tomorrow would just have to do.

Being somewhat of a night owl, Anne always enjoyed reading in bed before going to sleep. Derrick, on the other hand, was gone the minute his head hit the pillow. This night was just like any other . . . or was it?

The day before, Derrick had gone to the store and purchased a copy of the book Anne was currently reading, and that afternoon he had replaced her copy with the one he had bought. Only this one had a little surprise in it. About fifteen pages beyond where Anne had stopped reading last night he had carved a perfectly shaped little niche for the stunning emerald ring he had bought her to celebrate the beginning of a new year together.

As Derrick climbed into bed, Anne had just picked up the book and started reading. He put his head on the pillow, closed his eyes, and a few minutes later heard her laugh in pure pleasure. She exclaimed, "Oh my gosh! You are the most wonderful man in the whole world!" as she grabbed him and began to shake him.

He rolled over with a dumb, sleepy look on his face and said, "Happy New Year, sweetheart" . . . then pulled out the champagne and two glasses he had stashed under the bed.

The Easter Bunny Strikes Again!

When my husband and I were children, we attended the same grade school in a small Iowa town. Every year at Easter our teachers would make up little baskets for each child, and every day a different child would have a basket hidden somewhere in the room. In it would always be some little treasure chosen especially for that child. It was a tradition that we all loved and looked forward to every year.

Our Easters for our own children have been made special by this tradition year after year, but as our two daughters grew older it became harder and harder to surprise them with something special. The usual candy was accepted with delight, but we wanted to make this a tradition that stuck with them with a true "treasure" to remember each year.

I had the brilliant idea of adding some tiny diamond chip earrings to each basket when the girls were eleven and thirteen, and my husband thought the idea was terrific. I found just the right earrings and eagerly awaited the excitement of our daughters on Easter Sunday.

Funny, though, on Easter Sunday there were half a dozen little baskets sitting on the table, and I had prepared only two! What was going on?

I handed the girls their baskets, and both my husband and I were pleased that they were so happy with their special gifts. They immediately put the earrings on and exclaimed they felt like princesses.

My husband turned to me and said, "Now it's your turn to find your treasure, honey!" as he handed me a basket. Beneath the malted milk eggs and jelly beans I found a perfect little sapphire, unset and waiting to join the three other matching sapphires I found in the other baskets.

"Honey, I wanted this to bring back the memories of how wonderful it was to find your own personal treasure for Easter, and I want to thank you for being MY Easter treasure every year. Tomorrow we'll go pick out a special setting to put these in."

Carriage Ride

Walking through the Old Town district of Scottsdale, Arizona each year during our winter vacation is always a favorite activity of mine. My husband David and I wander for hours, holding hands, window shopping, and stopping for coffee at pretty little sidewalk cafés. It's especially romantic in the early evenings as white Christmas lights come on all around us and fountains surrounded by beautifully sculpted stallions fill the air with the sound of rushing water.

We've been married a long, long time, and I know I'm a lucky woman to have a husband who still holds my hand everywhere we go and truly enjoys our time together no matter what we're doing.

But, every year I ask David if we can go for a ride in one of the carriages that tours the streets, and that's been the one wish he hasn't granted me. I really can't blame him because he's more than likely anticipating a sneezing attack from being in such close proximity to a horse, but I ask anyway just in case he changes his mind.

A horse-drawn carriage passed by, and I smiled sweetly up at him. "David dear, could we just do a short carriage ride this year? It would be so romantic." Imagine my surprise when this time he simply said, "Sure honey. Next one that goes by we'll flag him down."

We strolled down the sidewalk slowly and, sure enough, when the next carriage passed David flagged him down. I was more than a little surprised, but I didn't say anything.

We climbed up into the carriage, and David asked the driver if he could do a modified trip that would last just a short time — and I laughed when David let out a great big sneeze as he finished his request to the driver! "Honey, we don't have to do this if you're going to be miserable," I told him.

"No, we're on our way, and I'll be just fine!" he replied, with another big sneeze.

I sat curled in the comfort of David's arm as we rode through the beautiful streets, content just to be close and warm with my husband. David bent down and kissed my forehead, and when I looked up at him I saw that he was holding his hand toward me with something draped across it. It was dark in the carriage so I bent close to look.

In his hand was a heart-shaped diamond pendant that I had admired earlier in the evening while we were window shopping. I didn't even know he'd gone back to the store!

"Honey, I want to give you this necklace as a reminder of how much I love being with you, no matter where we are or what we're doing. I decided to give it to you on this carriage ride because I really want you to know that I'll go anywhere with you or for you." And he ended with a great big sneeze!

I wear the necklace all of the time, and because of the love he shared when he gave it to me it has a more special meaning to me than any other gift he has ever given me.

Fish story

My husband and I are avid fishermen; sometimes I think it's the only reason he married me! On weekends we load up our fishing equipment, a picnic basket full of goodies, and head for our favorite "fishin' hole".

Now, this isn't a secluded spot, mind you. We most often fish from the dock at a nearby bait and tackle shop. They say we're good advertising because we always catch fish. We're often surrounded by bait shop patrons asking us how we're doing and what bait we're using.

As luck would have it on this particular day, I was catching fish right and left and my husband was having nothing but trouble with lost bait, snags, and fish that just "almost" got caught. He seemed sort of off kilter, but I told him to try to relax and enjoy the day.

Finally, after fiddling with a snag for some time and then throwing down his pole in disgust, he grumbled something about getting a soda out of the cooler and stalked off. This was so unlike his usual even temperament that I decided to go after him, but first I stopped to pick up his pole so no one would trip over it.

Imagine my surprise as I lifted the pole and got clunked on the head by a diamond ring tied neatly in place of the sinker. I had to look twice, and then started laughing when I realized that all of my husband's aggravation had been meant to lead me to exactly this point. I turned and looked to see him standing in the doorway of the bait shop, employees, owner, and a few patrons all peeking around him with big grins on their faces.

"Hey honey! Have I told you lately that I sure like fishin' with you?" No special occasion, just a very fitting way to tell me how much he loves me.

Go West Young Woman

*I*t had taken a couple of weeks of negotiation, but Joe finally got the deal he wanted and drove out of the dealership in his brand new Explorer.

His wife Mary had been a little skeptical with his reasoning that the purchase was because their kids who were now fourteen and sixteen, would be taking long trips with them in the car and they needed more room. He knew she was on to him . . . his real motivation for buying a utility vehicle was because he loved to go four-wheeling on Saturdays with his friends and felt a little conspicuous when he was always doing the "riding" and never the driving.

Joe arrived home and ran into the house as excited as a nine-year-old boy with his first bicycle. Mary was working at her computer as Joe came up behind her, gave her a big kiss on the cheek and said, "C'mon, c'mon, let's go! Let's go for a ride."

They jumped into the Explorer and headed out of town. After a few minutes, Joe pulled over to the side of the road and invited Mary to drive. She got behind the wheel and found that she really enjoyed the sensation of sitting up so high with a great view of everything ahead of her.

Joe instructed, "Hang a left here," and as Mary followed his directions she found herself heading into the late afternoon sun. To shield her eyes, she quickly reached up and pulled down the visor. She felt something "plop" right into her lap and then roll onto the floor of the truck. "What was that?" she exclaimed.

"I don't know. Better pull over and let's check it out."

Once they were pulled over on a side road, Mary found a little blue velvet box on the floor and looked over at Joe quizzically. "What's this?"

Sporting a foolish grin, Joe just shrugged his shoulders. Mary opened the box to find an alligator pendant with ruby chips for its eyes. "Oh my gosh! What's this all about?" she exclaimed with great pleasure.

"Well, honey, I just wanted to say thank you for your understanding about my buying this vehicle. We could've lived without it, but you knew how much it meant to me. You're a wonderful wife, and I don't tell you often enough how much I appreciate you. Thank you."

Mary leaned over to hug Joe and said, "You're the best Joe. I'm just happy you're happy!"

Repair Shop Romeo

My boyfriend, Jason, is a mechanic who I met when I was going through a series of car repairs that I was beginning to think were going to drive me into bankruptcy. He kept assuring me that my car was worth repairing and that it would cost me less in the long run than buying a new car. So I just kept following his advice until finally the day arrived that he pronounced my car "as good as new".

Jason is very shy, but as car repairs threw us together over and over, I began to see that he was a very good, honest person. I liked him more and more but wasn't sure how to approach him, so I just kept visiting with him and finding out more about him each time I went into his shop.

On the day he announced that he had done everything he could to my car, I felt a little sad, but I still couldn't bring myself to suggest to Jason that we see each other outside of his work.

I got in my car slowly, battling with my desire to see Jason socially and my fear of rejection. I turned to wave at him standing in the doorway of the shop and sat down in my car — or tried to sit down. I landed on something bulky in the seat and got back up to see what was there.

A teddy bear! Complete with jaunty hat and a colorful scarf around his neck. He was just so cute, and I knew Jason must have put him there. I picked him up and saw that there was an envelope hanging from his scarf, so I pulled it off and opened it. I never once turned around to look at Jason. I was too afraid I'd do something completely silly!

Inside the envelope I found a dainty little gold necklace with a simple heart charm. The note that was included read, "Turn around, and I'll be there. But, if you get into your car and drive away, I'll have your answer."

Of course I turned around and found myself practically nose to nose with Jason. He took the necklace from my hand and held it up between us. "Melinda, you're the nicest girl I've met in a long time. I just didn't know how to ask you out.

But I knew I couldn't let you get away from me. Will you wear this necklace when we go out to dinner together?"

That was the beginning of our relationship. Once Jason became comfortable with me, his romantic nature showed itself again and again. But it's the gold heart hanging on a chain that truly won MY heart.

Important Dates

*F*or a life together continuously filled with love, romance, and self preservation, insert your important dates to remember below:

Our First Date: _____

The Day We Got Engaged: _____

Our Wedding Anniversary: _____

Her Birthday: _____

Valentines Day: February 14th (Never! Never! Never! forget this day!)

Other important reminders: _____

_____

To err is human except when important dates are involved . . . then it can become downright miserable!

Keep the Romance Growing . . .

Help us keep love and romance flourishing. Tell us how you (or someone you know) have created or participated in the giving of a gift of jewelry for a special occasion and your story may be featured in our next book.

Include the following information with your story:

Name, Address, City, State, Zip, Telephone Number, E-mail Address

Mail your story to: Richardson Resource Group
PMB 345, 8711 E. Pinnacle Peak Rd.
Scottsdale, AZ 85255
FAX: 480-451-9372

We will make sure that you and the author are credited for your contribution and receive an autographed copy of the book.

Thank you for your participation in our efforts to promote love and romance.

We wish you much romance,

Dave & Jean